THE

Heart

WARRIOR

I know what He's done for me!

PASTOR TERESA TAYLOR

To order additional copies of this book, contact:
Xlibris
844-714-8691
www.Xlibris.com
Orders@Xlibris.com

ISBN: Softcover   978-1-6641-8492-3
        EBook   978-1-6641-8491-6

Print information available on the last page

Rev. date: 11/10/2021

DEDICATION

Baby, you will never know the Love I have for you and the joy you brought into my life the day we became one. God certainly knew what He was doing when He joined us together; as the scripture states,

"Wherefore they are no more twain, but one flesh.
What therefore God hath joined together,
let not man put asunder."
Matthew 19:6

It is my heart's desire that we continue to do the work of the Lord as we grow old together, My Sweet Taylor.

CONTENTS

FOREWORD

As the author, Teresa shares her personal experience in this book that demonstrates her faith and how God manifested himself in her life. Teresa's life has shown others to have that same faith when they face similar situations.

This book encourages and inspires those who need lifting and are waiting for a turnaround in their lives. However, there are some tear-jerking moments that you will encounter. The way that Teresa fought this battle is unbelievable. She never complained as some of us do, nor did she give up, no matter how hard things seemed. Teresa is a fighter, a warrior, and she aggressively took back everything that the enemy tried to steal from her; her joy, peace, and body.

In this book, you will learn how to deal with different life circumstances that come your way. You will learn how to wait on God's timing for your breakthrough, healing, and restoration. Waiting on God is not an easy thing to do, especially when we want to do things our own way and in our own time. Our timing is not God's timing. However long it takes, God doesn't make mistakes, and He allows different circumstances in our lives to help us mature in Him and tell of His goodness of how we can make it. Sometimes those circumstances are not pleasant to us. However, they are good for us.

I can remember growing up as a kid with Teresa. Teresa witnessed to me about Christ, but I wasn't ready for Teresa's level, especially as a child. I really can't remember Teresa being any other way. She didn't show up to school one day and say, "I gave my life to Christ." No. Teresa was a Christian when I met her. Teresa was always on point and was different from all other friends. Teresa didn't get into fights like the rest of us. Teresa loved God and was souled out for Jesus. As kids, we thought it was odd that Teresa would act and dress a certain way. It was the GOD in her that was different. She was set apart for God's use, which was something we could not understand as children. However, Teresa was well respected, as she is now.

In the end, Teresa demonstrates that if we just keep focused on God, He will see us through, and we will win and have the victory.

Louann Overstreet

INTRODUCTION

Have you ever wondered why things happen in your life as they do? It seems like you must take the long way around. Let me tell my story and give my testimony.

On February 14, 1966, in a small town named Albany, Ga, the time had finally come for me to be born. I want to think that for my parents, Woodall Terry and Frances Terry, this was a day filled with joy, laughter, and excitement. Little did my mom know that the child she had birthed into this world would become a woman who loves God with every fiber of her being, and through the ups and downs, she would faithfully serve Christ.

As I grew up, I can remember our parents would always ensure that we went to church and went to school. The very first church my family became members of was Mt. Calvary Baptist Church of Lee County, Ga., and our pastor's name was Reverend Roland Jenkins. I can recall my father being ordained a deacon, and my mother was ordained a deaconess of the church. Working in the church was especially important to our parents, and they taught us the significance of being obedient to God and the leaders in the church.

Our father thought it would be nice to start a gospel singing group with me and my three sisters, Sangra, Betty, and Tan, called "The Terry Sisters."

We all had a love for music. Our father chose me to be the lead singer because I could hold notes for a long time. One of the songs we would always sing when asked was, "I kept on searching." We would visit different churches in surrounding cities close to where we lived, singing about Jesus, but did not really have a relationship with Jesus. I now know that whatever you do for Christ, let it be real.

Scripture encourages us:
"And whatsoever ye do, do it heartily,
as to the Lord, and not unto men."
Colossians 3:23

CHAPTER 1

The Different One

School was easy for me, and I enjoyed attending. In the 1ˢᵗ grade, I was tested for the gifted program and was placed in the 2ⁿᵈ grade. My sisters and I were members of the Girls Club, where we became players on the basketball team. It was so much fun to be on the team and be a group of girls coming together to learn life lessons and skills.

I was born different. When my mom had me in the hospital, people thought I was so pretty; my Aunt Pat and Aunt Sharon have a dispute going even now as to which one of them named me "Punkin" because they say I look like a pretty pumpkin. Let me say this; it does not matter to me which one of you named me; I simply adore both of my aunts for different reasons.

Aunt Sharon, you know, growing up, you were the Auntie that my sisters and I loved going to your house to play in your makeup. Our mom would not allow us to wear it, but, oh what fun that would be. Aunt Pat, you were the Auntie that allowed me to come over to your house and stay. You made me feel safe after I was molested. I will always be grateful to you for being there for me.

As a youth, my father molested me. That is an event I will never forget. Being molested leaves you questioning, "Why me?" "Why did you do that?" and "How could you?" are just a few of the many questions children who are molested ask. As I look back over my life, I realize it is all a part of the story I am telling.

I know what He's done for me.

My father pushed me on the bed and started to touch my breast. I knew that was not right, so I begged him not to do it. He told me that I better not tell anyone what he was doing, but I took my hands and hit him as hard as I could and ran to tell my Nannie. She called my mom, who was at work, and told her what had happened. When she came home, she asked what took place, and I told her. She took me over to my Aunt Pat's house, where I stayed for a while. I remember having fun with my cousins while I was there and not really thinking about what had happened. But then the day came when I had to go back home. I was so afraid when both my parents came to get me. In my mind, I just knew it would happen again, but it did not. He apologized to me and said it would not happen again.

Molestation is the "sexual assault or abuse of a person, especially a woman or a child." Many families are going through this same situation to this day. I encourage everyone reading this; if you have been molested or know someone who has and you have not told anyone, please do so NOW! I also want to say that when an individual has been molested, the perpetrator makes the victim feel as if it is their fault, but I am here to tell you that it is not true. Talking with survivors of sexual assault should come from being a supportive person and a non-judgmental standpoint, and a lot of times, the victim needs a listening ear.

CHAPTER 2

The Early Years

Growing up, I was always inquisitive about everything, wanting to know why this and why that. I can recall one time while my mother worked as a short-order cook at a diner called *The Hasty House*. Lord, I loved to go there and have her cook me a patty melt and some fries. My grandmother, whom we called, "Nannie" was keeping us at the time. I can remember this story so vividly in my mind. I was outside playing in her backyard when I noticed her placing clothes in the washing machine. The machine caught my attention. The washing machine was the kind that you had to thread the clothes through a ringer to get the water out. I know some of you reading this remember the type of machine I am referring to is called a Wringer Washing Machine.

Well, as I watched my grandmother performing this task, in my young mind, I thought, "I wonder what would happen if I tried placing my arm through the wringer." As you might guess, it did not turn out well. I started screaming to the top of my lungs, "Nannie Nannie!" She came running, saying, "Child, what have you done?" I had to go to the hospital, and they put my arm in a cast; that was no fun. My arm itched all the time, and I could not get inside the cast to scratch it. To get some relief, I would get a ruler, place it down in the cast, and rub my arm; that was me being different. My great-grandmother said, "I bet you won't want to try that again," and believe me, I never did.

My sisters and I did a lot of different things in school. I was in the 4H club, I was chosen Senior Superlative, my sister Betty and I played the clarinet together in the band, and she was selected as section leader. Jean (Sangra) was in the chorus; Tan was also in the band; she played the flute, and Terri wanted to play basketball because she is so tall. I would sign up to be in every talent show because I love singing, my sister Betty was in the Miss Albany High School pageant where she played the piano, and my sister Jean was also a debutant. My oldest brother, Randy, loves to play the piano, and Woodall enjoys playing his bass guitar, so you can see we are a musically inclined family.

Our mom worked two jobs to ensure that we could take part in any activity we wanted. I am so wonderfully blessed with a mother who not only was there for us, but she prayed for us, played with us, took us to church, and most importantly, she lives a life of Godliness before us. Our great example of how to be a loving, caring, considerate and GREAT COOK comes from our dear mom. Mom, please know that you are loved more than you could ever know. I thank the Lord every day for allowing me to have such a dear mother. When we were young, I remember how you would bring children who were hungry home and feed them. The example she showed us was scripture-based.

"But do not forget to do good and to share, for
with such sacrifices God is well pleased."
Hebrews 13:16

That was how she showed her love for the Lord and his people. I try to do this daily because I love the Lord, and I want Him to be pleased with my life.

Now I must say, I did not always do what was right. I recall my senior year in high school. I got a job at Kentucky Fried Chicken (KFC) as a prep worker, and during my senior year in high school, I was able to clock out of school at noon during my last semester. I did well enough in school that I only went to school from August to December, and that was it for me until the end of the school year when I came back to have practice for my graduation.

I used the money I made by working to pay for a little Chevy Monza. Lord, did I love that car. I put a sign on the front of it that read "Lady T." My mom and dad helped me with the down payment. I was proud of myself for making that purchase. Going to work and saving money for something you can call your own is a sign of maturity.

As the school year was ending, we had what you call "Senior Skip Day" oh boy, here comes trouble. All the seniors decided to go to Irwin Co. Georgia to a beach called Crystal Beach. My mom told me not to go, but baby, I had a car, and I was going. To everyone reading this, I found out that day:

"Children obey your parents in the Lord, for this is right."
Ephesians 6:1.

I drove onto the beach and got my car stuck in the sand; yep, I had to have it towed. Believe it or not, I got away with it. Well, almost.

On senior day, the parents were invited to come to the senior program to see the things we had done throughout the year. We were given plaques, awards, certificates, and then everyone would watch a slide show presentation. Now I had no idea they would put the day my car got towed out of the sand on that slide show for my mother to see. Lord have mercy, she turned to me and said, "well, Sista, you've been found out." All I could do was hold my head down and pray, *Lord, don't let her take my car.* They didn't take it, but I could not drive it for a week.

CHAPTER 3

The Calling Upon My Life

Let's focus on what the call of God looks like to me. At the age of 18, I knew that the Lord was calling me, but I was not ready to surrender my all to Him. Looking back, even when I was a young girl, my life was different than most. My mom sheltered my sisters, Sangra, Betty, Tangela, Terri, and me from things she felt weren't good for our lives.

My parents believed in the Word of God, especially:

"Train up a child in the way he should go: and when he is old, he will not depart from it."
Proverbs 22:6

We were not allowed to go on dates, to the movies, nor were we allowed to attend sleepovers at neighbors' houses. These are just a few things I recall. Of course, we felt our parents were too strict. However, my mom would always say God commissioned her to raise her children differently. She told us that we had the lords anointing upon our lives, and she had to guard it. Nonetheless, when you are young and want to experience life, understanding the anointing was something we didn't feel was right. I finished high school and then went on to Albany State College. It has since been renamed to the great Albany State University home of the Golden Rams. I majored in Early Childhood Education with an emphasis in philosophy. I wanted to be an elementary school teacher. Some of the classes I took were English composition, elementary algebra, literature, and economics. My grades were decent, but I honestly could have made A's and B's if I tried harder. Unfortunately, I would miss classes to go and spend time with my boyfriend. I knew that wasn't a good idea since I was raised in the church and taught that fornication was a sin, but my flesh pulled me in.

Therefore, now that I'm older and have a relationship with Jesus Christ, I understand how important it is at an early age one should seek after the things of God.

The Bible states:
"Seek ye first the kingdom of God, and his righteousness,
and all these things shall be added unto you."
Matthew 6:33

Putting God and the things of God first will eventually get you your heart's desire. After hanging out so much with my boyfriend and being sexually active, I became pregnant. I was so ashamed of what I'd done. I didn't know how to tell my mother.

I thought I could hide it. I remember trying to hide my stomach by covering it up with my cape that I wore to prepare biscuits at work, but that didn't work. My mom knew; the Lord let her know.

During this time, I was still living at home, and my dad was so mad, he told my boyfriend we had to get married. We got married on my 19th birthday, which is Valentine's Day. The marriage was rocky from the start for many reasons. One reason was neither of us had a relationship with Christ. I had no idea my husband would change on me. He began to drink alcohol more and more. On the days that he didn't have to work, he would drink all day. It was causing so much friction in our home, and the entire situation was breaking my heart.

Our daughter, Lateshia, loved her dad so much and didn't like it when he would push and yell at me; she would cry, which made me feel so sad. My oldest sister and her husband lived in Atlanta, Ga. They didn't have any children at the time, so they would ask if Lateshia could come and stay with them sometimes, and I would let her go.

I would have to call and ask, "Hey can I get my child back" they truly had fallen in love with her, but you couldn't help it. The little girl was just straight beautiful. I remember how she had this big head with no hair, and I would pray, *Lord, please let her hair grow,* and boy did it grow. Even now that she's an adult, her hair is long.

When I got married, I was strictly in my flesh. I thought I knew what love was; however, I've come to realize you will never know true love until you have a relationship with Jesus Christ. There is a distinct difference between being in love and being in lust. Let me encourage someone who is considering getting married; please take time to date and get to know one another before getting married. There is much more to marriage than being intimate with someone. Find out all you can about that person. First and foremost, is that person a believer of Jesus Christ?

I wasn't saved when I got married, and neither was he, but we both believed in Jesus Christ. I must say believing in Jesus Christ but not having a relationship with him won't work. It takes a mind genuinely focused on the things of Christ and a heart that's clean and pure.

David said in the book of Psalms:
"Create in me a clean heart, O God;
and renew a right spirit within me."
Psalms 51:10

Since I've given my life to Christ, I have found out that it is of the utmost importance that I honor God in every area of my life. As I look back on my first marriage, I realize I should not have done it because neither of us was prepared. Marriage is hard, and it takes work from both parties. Now that I'm older, I understand that it's about giving 100 percent. You're both on the same team fighting together. At the time, my husband abused alcohol and would abuse me and curse me out without any concern for me or our daughter. I began to attend church more and more and eventually gave my life to Christ. I remember that day vividly because I cried all that day and two weeks afterward. My soul was truly sorrowful for the things I had done against the will of God. Before that unforgettable day when I received Jesus Christ as my Lord and Savior, I would go to church and pretend that I had a relationship with Christ. But, as soon as church was over, I would once again do things of the world, such as cursing, lying, and unforgiveness. It's so amazing that when I gave my life to Christ, He removed those things from me. I began to study the Word of God, and that is how I grew more in the ways of God.

The Bible emphasizes:
"Study to shew thyself approved unto God,
a workman that needed not to be ashamed,
rightly dividing the word of truth."
2 Timothy 2:15

CHAPTER 4

Maturing in Christ

I continued to attend church services, and the more I did, my husband didn't like it. One night I came home from a Friday night prayer service, and he put me out. As I drove up with my friend Evangelist Nancy Bailey, we could see my clothes on the back porch where he has placed them. I got out and tried to go into my house, but he opened the door and told me to go back to where I came from.

I was so embarrassed and hurt, but he made it clear that he was not ready to be a Christian, so I went to stay with my friend Nancy. She and I began to do prayer in her mobile home, where the Lord started becoming the focal point in my life. As I look back on my life, I realize that my living with Nancy taught me how to pray, seek the Lord for EVERYTHING, and have faith in God.

There is a story I often speak about because God proved Himself to us as two single women to:

*"**Trust in the** L**ord** **with all** thine **heart**, and lean not unto thine own understanding. **In all** thy ways acknowledge him, and he shall direct thy paths."*
Proverbs 3:5-6.

We lived in a small country city named Sasser Ga., which is about 18 minutes from a bigger city. Albany is where we were headed, to be exact. The car Nancy had was a burgundy Ford LTD, and it was a gas guzzler. However, we didn't have more than fifty cents between us, and most people wouldn't dream of taking that car anywhere. We prayed, asking the Lord to stretch the gas, and we made it to Albany on *fifty cents* worth of gas. My faith grew to another level in God. I've learned that God doesn't always fix your storm; he fixes you while you're in the storm. That's exactly what he did for me. After staying with my friend, Evangelist Nancy, for a while, I decided to go back home with my parents. But, I was still trying to make our marriage work.

What ended up happening is, I became pregnant with our second child, Kristen, who brought so much happiness into my life. I had no idea how this little precious anointed soul would be such a blessing in my life and so many other people's lives.

My biological father and mother had similar problems in their marriage. He was older than my mom and always being mean to her. I remember that her relationship with Christ caused a rift in their marriage, and he ended it. This is a teachable moment. Being equally yoked is the best thing for a marriage. I mean that both individuals need to make sure they are Christ-centered before joining together in marriage.

During all the trials with my marriage, my biological father died. The church became my solace during the pain I was facing in my marriage, and other situations life brings. My mom married again, and the man she married was a pastor who loved the Lord. Apostle Robert L. Brunson-loved my mom and ALL her children. He did not have any children of his own. He was such a true Man of God in every way. It's extremely hard for me to write this part of my story because I miss him dearly. From day one, he showed so much love to our family and was such a great provider to our mom.

He pastored a little church titled "Holy Temple Non- Denominational church, where he preached the truths of God's word without compromise. The church grew, so he relocated to another place on Radium Springs Road in Albany, Ga. The ministry continued to grow as people would travel from miles around to hear him preach. I grew stronger in my relationship with Christ and began to function in different church roles, such as a devotional leader; nowadays, it's referred to as worship leaders.

I took this position seriously. Oh, how I enjoyed leading the people of God into the presence of the Lord, and my soul was filled with such joy. My relationship with Christ was growing because I was in church ALL the time. In the '80s and '90s, people were in church for Sunday Praise and Worship, Monday Noon Day Prayer, Wednesday Noon Day Prayer, Friday Noon Day Prayer, Friday Night Testimony service, and Saturday choir rehearsal.

Sunday Church, we would go in at 9:30 am and come out at 3:00 go to the Buffett, usually Ryan's, Golden Corral, or good Ole Barnhills, then be back for 6:00 pm service. I say, "Try that now and see who stays." I believe that people go back into sin because they do not have a solid foundation in the Word of God.

David said in the book of Psalms:
"Thy word have I hid in mine heart,
that I might not sin against thee."
Psalms19:11

Spending time around other believers and people who have a love for God's things, such as yourself, will cause you to want more of His Word and less of the world. Simply put, the more of the Word of God that goes in you, the more the world comes out of you; the two cannot stay in the same place. When the light comes, the darkness goes.

I always felt comfortable calling our new dad, Dad. He was just so genuine. He believed in sharing, loving, and giving. I could go to him about anything, and I did. It had been some years since my first husband and I separated, so I asked my dad what I should do because my husband had moved on with someone else. We had a long discussion, and I decided to file for a divorce. It really took a toll on me because he would not help me financially with the children. My mom and dad allowed us to live with them until I could get myself together. I found a job working at a Convenience store named Woodall's. I worked the three to eleven shift while my parents kept my children, and I was so grateful to them for lending a helping hand. I worked there for a while; then, I was offered a job working at Kinder Kare Learning Center as a three-year-old teacher.

I genuinely enjoyed working with young people; they say the cutest things and love you unconditionally. I was still growing in Christ, attending church, raising my two children, who were getting older. Some men were asking me to date them during this time, but no one stood out. Life was happening, and I was enjoying working and traveling back and forth to Florida with my dad as he was a traveling evangelist. One week before Christmas, the Kinder Care Learning Center owner told us that would be our last week of work; they were closing that center.

I will never forget that Christmas because my children had the best Christmas; the Lord blessed them in a mighty way. He proved to me that no matter the circumstance, always trust Him to work them out.

Proverbs states:
"Trust in the LORD with all thine heart, and lean not unto
thine own understanding.⁶ In all thy ways acknowledge him,
and he shall direct thy paths."
Proverbs 3:5-6

I know what He's done for me.
I must say something about how sin can destroy
a home and a marriage, which is why Christ
should be the head of EVERY family.

As Matthew stated:

*"But **seek** ye **first the kingdom** of God, and his righteousness;*
*and all **the**se things shall be added unto you."*
Matthew 6:33

In today's world, He's not the head of a lot of homes, and divorces are at an all-time high. He wants to use families representing examples of love in the home, grace, forgiveness, and Christlike character. My dad, Apostle Brunson, always showed Christlike character in our home, in the church, and everywhere he would go, and the congregation loved him.

I would travel with him and open the services with song and prayer. Pastors would invite him to come and preach, but he would always seek the Lord as to which engagement to attend. I can recall a church in Sylvester, Ga., where Pastor Gloria Samuel, a mighty woman of God, went home to be with the Lord. She would preach the truths of God's word just like my dad.

I met my Goddaughter, Jolena, in another little church in Cordele, Ga. My dad loved the name of this church, Straight Life Church of God, Pastor Fredrick Williams. Lord, they loved to sing and praise the Lord in that church. Jolena, who was around 15 then, began to grow spiritually in her church as my father would come and preach. She often came to me and asked if I would pray with her concerning being a young Christian and mentoring her. It was such an honor to encourage her to stay the course, pray, read the Bible as often as possible while still in school, and help build her up in her most holy faith.

As I stayed in contact with her, the Lord gave me such love for her that eventually, I just started referring to her as my Goddaughter. As a daughter should, she became part of our family, and to this day, she's part of my journey. I do thank the Lord for her.

CHAPTER 5

Lessons Learned

Finally, I remarried. My second marriage taught me some huge lessons, and I want to help someone else not make the same mistakes. Do not marry someone you know deep down inside is not FULLY delivered from the world, and you think you can help them get saved. DON'T DO IT! It may start off rather good, the affection, the striving to make you happy, but then REAL-LIFE HITS! Having another baby coming into the picture when there is already not enough income can shake a new marriage.

Another lesson to learn in this is the importance of family planning. My Dad didn't believe in dating for an extended period because he said that leaves space for the enemy. This is true; however, when you are dating, no matter how long or short the "courtship" is, make sure there is a discussion about having children and caring for them financially. The bible encourages us to be good stewards of our monies.

My husband and I didn't discuss family planning, and we were certainly not financially equipped for another child. Nonetheless, we awaited the arrival of our next child. I prayed the Lord would let us have a son. He did just that, and our handsome little boy, Tyrun, was born.

My Dad was a Prophet of God. Webster's dictionary defines Prophet as *someone who publicly declares a message that he or she believed has come from God.* He told me that the Lord said to name our son Tyrun, and he gave me the spelling. Dad said the Lord would use Tyrun at an early age, and he would have a love for the Lord. Tyrun was a good child, and as he continued to grow, I had the privilege of taking him and my other children to work with me since I was the center's assistant director. Tyrun was walking at just a year old. His teacher told me that he would raise his hand and praise the Lord.

I was working, and my husband was working; life was going in the right direction. Then it happens, I got pregnant again with our child, Bethany. Lord, this little girl was gorgeous! I remember in the hospital, the nurses would bring her to me all swaddled with a pink ribbon in her hair, looking like a sweet peach. All went well with the delivery, so we went home and continued living and raising a family. We were living in a house we really couldn't afford, as my husband was between jobs. Even though we were still going to church, trials were happening.

The bible teaches:
*"Blessed is the man that endureth temptation: for when he is
tried, he shall receive the crown of life, which the Lord
has promised to them that love Him."*
James 1:2

I do love the Lord and have learned that trials are part of the work of God. The rent was just too much to pay, so we found a cheaper place.

I liked it better, we didn't have as many rooms, but we made it work. I can remember thinking my marriage was going well. I had been promoted to daycare director, and my husband had a decent job. We were attending church regularly, and I thought we are happy.

Apparently not.

I came home from work one Wednesday evening to find my husband attempting to molest my child. The feelings and thoughts that flooded my mind are just unexplainable. One thing I remember is saying to myself, "Lord, not the same thing to my child." He jumped up off her and said he was sorry, but that was just unacceptable. He immediately got his things and left.

My daughter and I discussed what happened. I told her that it was not her fault, I loved her, and we would get through this. We then got ready to go to church because it was our bible study night, and I was the devotional leader of the church who opened the service. Have you ever looked back over your life and regret certain decisions you made? This experience is one no parent should ever have to face, and how I handled the situation is one of those decisions I regret.

However, I know the Lord's Word encourages:
*"And we know that all things work together for good to them
that love God, to them who are the
called according to his purpose."*
Romans 8:28

I must say I didn't fully grasp what this scripture meant at the time, but during this trial, I learned that He does not create these situations, but He uses them to build our faith as we go through them. So, despite the good, the bad, and the ugly, God has taught me to give thanks in all and through all things.

The lessons in being single were upon me again. But, this time, it was me, the Lord, and four children. It wasn't easy raising children without a man in the house, and I know why God ordained marriage between a man and a woman. Each has their own role within the marriage, and as a parent. I was trying to teach my son how to do things that a father should teach a little boy, and it was challenging, but with the help of the Lord, I got it done. My children lacked attention from me because I spent a lot of time working to keep us afloat, and I would be tired when I got home; nonetheless, there was still more left to be done.

I remember many nights, when I went to my room, shut my door, and just sobbed; I wanted to scream. While I was at work, my daughter Lateshia called me and was crying, saying someone had broken into our house. Oh, my goodness, what more, Lord? I left quickly and went home to check on my children and the house to find that it was true. All their Christmas things had been stolen the week before Christmas. My heart was hurt again. Who would do this during the holidays? I called the police and my parents. The police began to do fingerprints inside and outside the house.

My parents stayed with us for a while, then they left. I was afraid to go to bed that night, but we eventually went off to sleep. I really didn't want to go to work the next day, but I did. I told my children I would be at the house when they got home so they would not be afraid. A few days after the break-in, I saw a man looking in as I was closing the shutters to my bedroom window. I called the police again. They checked the neighborhood and found no one. There certainly was a man looking in my room, and I had had enough. In addition to having to be Mom and Dad, I was still dealing with my daughter's trauma, making sure she was alright with what had gone on in her life. That was the final thing that made me decide to move away from the house where we lived. My assistant director, Tara Price, was such a special person in my life. God used her in many ways to be a blessing to my children and me.

She would take me to lunch, pay for my meal, buy the children clothes and give me money to help with groceries. She was certainly Heaven sent. She kept telling me that I should move to Lee County, where she lived, emphasizing that the schools were great for the children.

She and I had been looking through the paper, and we found a duplex in Lee County. It was privately owned; the owner was genuinely nice and allowed me to move in. When the children saw it, they loved it! Let me tell you, the Lord blessed us with such a beautiful place, and I just got a raise on my job, so the Lord knew I could handle it.

CHAPTER 6

A Change Is Coming

I was growing spiritually and enjoying all His blessings. I purchased a new car from the dealership, a 1999 Ford Sable Wagon with plenty of room for the children and me. We drove to Ohio with my Mom and Dad to visit his family, and, oh, what fun we had! We went to Kings Island amusement park in Mason, Ohio. The children enjoyed themselves immensely. I still can't believe I drove that far by myself with four children, but my Dad often stopped to let us all rest. My oldest daughter, Tia, was helping with her younger siblings. She would help them to the bathroom and assist with holding their hands at the park. She was a wonderful big sister.

When I think about this time, it assures me that God sees our future because the new position I had came with bonuses for the employee that kept their daycare center on budget. Each year we were given a budget. Staying within those numbers would be rewarded with a bonus at the end of the year.

My family loves to travel, and we did quite a bit of it. Every year, the company I worked for had a candy fundraiser competition, and the center director who sold the most candy won a cash prize. The winning directors also could bring their families on a company-sponsored trip to the Holiday Inn Sun Spree Resort in Panama City Beach, Florida, with the hotel expenses paid. That yearly trip became a great part of our lives. My children and I enjoyed going there because the directors would bring their families and we would all have lots of fun while getting to know everyone. After the weekend, we would all go back to our homes and continue living our lives.

During the summertime, while planning our Church's Pastor's Appreciation, it was my task to do the publicity for the event one year. So I went to our local radio station, WJYZ, and spoke with the radio station personality Frank C. I had taken announcements there before, so we began talking, just catching up on life. While we were conversing, another radio personality, Eric Taylor, came from the back of the station and asked Frank to introduce me. After Frank introduced us, we talked a little more before I had to be on my way.

One Sunday after church, my children and I went to get us some Chinese food. As I walked into the restaurant, there he was, Eric, the radio personality that I had met at the station. My daughter, Lateshia, came in with me to help with the meals. He thought Lateshia was my sister; as we were chatting, I told him she was my daughter. We talked a little about church and what we both had planned for the rest of that day. He left, and my daughter and I placed our order.

As time went on, my family prayed that the Lord would bless me with a spouse to help me raise my children. They were all going through different stages, especially Tyrun. He needed a father in his life, so as God would have it, one day, I was at work preparing to place a food order for the center when the phone rang. It was Eric. He wanted to know if I would let him take me to lunch one day.

I thought he was playing, and I told him, "stop playing; you do not want to date me."

He said, "honestly, I really want to take you to lunch."

So, I said, "yes, I will go with you to lunch."

I couldn't wait to tell my parents that I had a lunch date! We went to Tifton, Ga., to eat at Applebee's. He and I talked for hours about our individual lives, our relationship with Christ, our jobs, just one thing after the other. It was a wonderfully comfortable and easy lunch.

We continued to talk every day after that. One night, I attended choir rehearsal because our church was getting ready to travel to Tampa, Florida, for a revival. He called me in the middle of rehearsal, and I stepped out to answer the call. I remember when I would hear his voice on the phone, my heart would feel so happy.

He ALWAYS brings a smile to my face. During our getting to know one another, he shared that one of his favorite female gospel artists was Helen Balor; she was also one of my favorites. He was searching for one of her songs to play, and it so happened that I had a copy of her CD. I told him that I would bring it by the station for him when I returned from my trip. I had to end the conversation and go back to practice. He asked if he could call me when I got home, and I said he could. I will never forget that night because we talked until 4 in the morning. Talking to him was so easy, and we both were so excited about all the things we had in common. Before we knew it, the time had gone so fast, and I had to travel to Tampa 2 hours later. I had to finish packing, so he and I said good night, and he asked me to please call him when I got there.

I was so happy and sleepy the entire ride to Tampa as I reminisced about the talk we had that night. I tried calling him to let him know we made it safely, but I couldn't reach him. Church services were so powerful, and people were giving their lives to Christ. My Dad was allowing the Lord to use him mightily to prophesy to the people of God. Dad was doing quite a bit of traveling and preaching the gospel during that time. The body of Christ was tremendously blessed during those revivals.

As we prepared to come back home, I tried to call Eric again but still no answer. I said, "now he told me to call him, and he's not answering his phone. Oh well, I'll handle this when I get home." So, here's the funny part, when I got in my car to check and make sure I was dialing the correct number, I realized I was not! All that time, I was dialing the wrong number! I called him while driving home and told him what happened and what I had said. He laughed and said, "I thought you didn't want to talk to me anymore."

Of course, that was the furthest thing from my mind. I was just so glad to speak with him, and we talked through the whole ride back home. It didn't take long for us to discuss the subject of marriage. Eric told me he had previously thought he would never marry a woman with multiple children, but I was different, and he had changed his mind. At the time, he was a sound tech at his church, and I was a praise leader at mine, so we would discuss what it would take for one of us to make a church change.

There are topics to talk about when you're dating, so you will know where each person stands with their beliefs. Which church to attend is only one of many. One Sunday, I looked up, and to my surprise, he was walking down the aisle of my church. I was so happy to see him. We went out to dinner and talked about the church service and my family. He said he really enjoyed the message that was delivered that day.

Even though things were going well with Eric and me, I felt like I was still being tested because my Dad had begun to get sick. He was diagnosed with congestive heart failure, and it was becoming hard for him to continue to preach and do a lot of traveling. My Mom helped him learn to eat healthier foods as he was going back and forth to the doctor for different tests. It had become extremely difficult for him to breathe because he was obese, and fluid would build up around his heart. I would pray and ask the Lord to please heal his body. His condition grew worse, but we all still prayed and continued to hold the faith for his healing. I was so thankful to have Eric in my life because he would encourage me that everything would be alright. I want to share something I've learned over the years about life and death.

Scripture tells us:
"We are confident, I say, and willing rather to be absent
from the body and to be present with the Lord."
2 Corinthians 5:8 (KJV)

CHAPTER 7

A Three Strand Cord

My Dad would appear to be doing well at times, and he and my Mom, along with my sister, Betty, and her husband, would travel for short vacations to allow him to get some rest and relaxation. While they were gone, he would leave me in charge of the church. I remember doing devotional service and ministering the Word of God a lot during this part of my life. My relationship with Christ was everything to me, and I would do a lot of fasting, praying, and seeking the face of God.

This is where I like to tell single women to get busy doing the work of the Lord, and when you look up, God has sent your spouse, and you are too busy working in the Kingdom to know.

Eric was such a sweet person, and most of all, he loved the Lord. I loved that he would always keep a song of worship in his heart and would just be humming. I knew that he was becoming incredibly special to me, and I could see myself being with him for the rest of my life. One time, my dryer stopped working, and if you have multiple children, you know how important it is to have a working dryer. I told Eric about it, and he asked if he could come over to my apartment and look at it.

Now this is where I want to talk about practicing abstinence. I firmly believe in God's Word, which teaches us to flee fornication and abstain from ALL appearances of evil. To me, that means there should not be any sexual relations happening while you are dating. Eric and I discussed our beliefs about the subject, and he, who is also a believer, did not have a problem with us not coming together sexually until we were married.

He looked at the dryer and said he knew a guy who worked on dryers. He would have him come by and look at it, so I gave him my key. At work the next day, I was thinking about how I would pay the guy if he could fix the dryer. Mr. Eric, as the children called him, met me at my house when I got off work to tell me the guy fixed the dryer, and he paid him, and I didn't owe him anything. All I could do was cry and tell the Lord and Eric, "thank you."

I know what He's done for me.

The children had started asking me when he would come over to our place. I didn't believe in having different gentlemen callers coming to my house before my children, especially my girls. I decided to allow him to come over one evening, and he asked if he could cook us a spaghetti supper. I love to tell this story because it took him so long to cook, and the kitchen was a mess, but the food was exceptional. The children talk about it even now.

The children and I had started feeling more comfortable with him coming over, so he would stop by, and we would watch movies together and have long talks. It was simply good Christian fun.

Christmas was coming, and he told me he wanted to give me money to help purchase the children some things. I thought that was nice of him, and once again, the Lord was making a way for me.

Shortly after Christmas, to my surprise, Eric had gone and asked my Dad for my hand in marriage. I found out after he proposed. I was at work one day, and Eric came in smiling. I didn't know that he had talked with my assistant, Tara, and my family about how he wanted to propose to me over the radio. Well, that didn't happen. He said he was too nervous. So, he came into the back of the daycare center, where I was, got on his knees, and asked if I would marry him.

Of course, I said, "Yes." He gave me the most beautiful white gold ring and flowers. The teachers were so happy for us, and they were smiling and congratulating us. My family was extremely excited, and everyone wanted to know when the wedding date would be.

Eric lived in an apartment, and his lease was up at the end of December. So, we found a duplex around the corner from where I was living, and we decided that he would move in there when his lease expired. The children and I would move in after we got married on January 28, 2001.

My staff gave me a beautiful bridal shower with some nice gifts, and the directors had a celebratory dinner for me where I received more gifts. Eric and I both decided that since this was the third time each of us was getting married, we wouldn't have a big wedding. Although my Dad was hospitalized shortly after we set a wedding date, God is good, and he was released from the hospital a week before the wedding.

Dad married us after church on January 28, 2001, with my family, friends, and some co-workers in attendance. This time around, we committed to allowing Christ to be the center of our marriage, as the word of the Lord emphasizes.

"Two are better than one; because they have a
good reward for their labour.
For if they fall, the one will lift up his fellow: but woe to him
that is alone when he falleth;
for he hath not another to help him up.

Again, if two lie together, then they have heat:
but how can one be warm alone?
And if one prevails against him, two shall withstand him;
and a threefold cord is not quickly broken."
Ecclesiastes 4:6-12 (KJV)

The God's Knot symbolizes the joining of one man, one woman, and God into a marriage relationship standing together to conquer and win in the marriage. We went out to eat afterward, then went home. Our life together had started, and we both were so happy.

Once we got married, I had time to fix our place like I wanted, making a happy home for my family. Eric and I had discussed having children while we dated, and I told him I didn't want to have any more children, but his take was we needed to have a child together. Although he had two children and I had four, he insisted on us having one together. I can say that he believed in saving money and being a good steward over what God entrusted into his hands.

We had been married about four months when I became pregnant. I remember so well because it was May of 2001, and I was giving the end-of-the-year speech to the pre-k class. When I finished, I dashed to the restroom to throw up. I stood looking in the mirror, saying, "Oh, Lord, I'm pregnant. One of the parents I was standing by at the ceremony had on a perfume that was so loud, I had to run back to the restroom again. I just couldn't be around loud scents. I didn't feel well the rest of that day. When I got home, I told Eric what happened, and he asked, "Do you think you might be pregnant?"

A few days later, Eric and I went to Walmart with my parents, and he and my Mom insisted I take a pregnancy test. I did not want to take a test because I told myself that I might not be pregnant, but truthfully the way I was feeling; I knew something was wrong. They said, "if you think you are not pregnant, then take the test and prove it." I took the test, and yes, the results showed positive. He was happy, and so was my Mom. I wasn't as happy because I became extremely sick with nausea during my past pregnancies, and I felt I was too old to be pregnant; I was 38 at the time. Nevertheless, we went home and told the children. They were excited to have another sibling in the family.

CHAPTER 8

The Sickness Begins

This pregnancy was quite different. I was 38 years old, and age plays a factor when you're having a baby later in life. I had to have an amniocentesis test done to check on the baby's health, and it came back fine. The doctor appointments went well each time, but I had a rough time with fatigue and not being able to hold food down in the beginning. I can recall one Sunday we were out to dinner, and in the middle of the meal, I began to vomit right there on the table. Believe me, I really did try not to, but it just came up and out. Our son Erik, bless his heart, would try so hard to help me. When I would eat, he would run and get a small trash can and sit by me because he knew I would vomit. I love you, Erik!

I had to take medication for nausea and vomiting. I remember how one of the meds was not working, so I needed a different one. We had to wait until my husband's insurance kicked in before we could afford to get it. He had changed his insurance, and there was a waiting period on the new policy. Oh, how I remember the day my husband got the medicine. I don't know who was more excited, him or me. The vomiting was hard on my family because they hated seeing what I was going through. Nearly every time I tried to eat, five minutes after I'd think it is down, I was hollering, "somebody get me a trash can." Our children talk about this turmoil to this day, only now they laugh about it.

After the medicine got in my system, I was able to eat and hold food down. I am so thankful for the Word of God. I prayed and read the Word a great deal to help me through that ordeal.

The Lord emphasizes that he will comfort us, and we can rest in Him.

"Come unto me, all ye that labor and are heavy
laden, and I will give you rest.
Take my yoke upon you and learn of me; for I am meek and
lowly in heart: and ye shall find rest unto your souls.
For my yoke is easy, and my burden is light."
Matthew 11:28-30

This was one scripture that caused me to hang on in there and know that God's abiding presence was always with me. I went into the hospital on January 14, 2002, and gave birth to our last son Joshua Taylor. During the delivery, I had to have oxygen because Joshua kept going into distress; however, I had a good delivery. Joshua was taken to the nursery for a while for observation because he breathed in some amniotic fluid. To God Be the Glory, he was fine, and we went home a few days later. Joshua and I were able to settle into a good nursing routine.

About a month later, on February 14, to be exact, my birthday, the company I worked for at the time, Children's Friend Learning Center gave me a birthday luncheon at Longhorns in Albany, Ga. I will never forget that day. My supervisor, Lisa Patterson, asked me to walk with her to her car to get the baby gift that she and my area directors had for me. The walk to her car felt like a country mile. I thought I was going to pass out; it was so hard for me to breathe. Every step was so tiresome. When I got home, I told my husband, "Baby, I'm sick; I can hardly breathe." He immediately said, "let's go to the ER," and we did.

After running tests, they admitted me to the hospital and told me I had postpartum cardiomyopathy, which is a form of heart failure, and thus the journey of my heart begins. I started going to a cardiologist, Dr. Steven Mitchell and an Internal Medicine Doctor, Sterling Barrett. They began treating me with heart failure medicines such as carvedilol, Cozaar, Furosemide, and Torsomide, to name a few. These are well-known medications that doctors administer to patients who have heart problems. Once I started on the medicines, I began to feel better. But, because I continued to eat unhealthy foods and suffered from being obese, that is not good for congestive heart failure patients. It is so easy to sit and eat fried foods, sugary sweets, starchy foods, and then when you look around, the weight has come upon you. I had to go in and out of the hospital quite frequently because it was hard for me to breathe. While in the hospital, there were many times they would pull so many liters of fluid off my body. I would go home feeling so much better, then turn around and still not eat right, so I'd have to make another trip to the hospital. I've learned that we often bring sickness upon us many times in our lives because we do not treat our bodies right.

Even the bible teaches us that practicing moderation is a good discipline. As a Christian, I look to God's word, and sure enough, the Good Book says that the Holy Spirit will produce self-control in your life.

"But the fruit of the Spirit is love, joy, peace, forbearance,
kindness, goodness, faithfulness,
gentleness, and self-control."
Galatians 5:22-23 (NIV)

I tried to work during all this sickness, but it really became hard to do because I was always so tired and fatigued. I would go to church and lead devotional services, but my clothes would be drenched in sweat when I was done. Nonetheless, I continued to do the work of the Lord.

My Dad was back in the hospital during this time, too. He was going to dialysis for his heart and kidneys, and Mom was right by his side every day. She loved him so much and did all that she could do for him, including helping run the church.

As a family, we were still blending and getting to know one another fully. Eric and I would have arguments sometimes as new couples do. I remember one time during a disagreement; he got so mad that he hit the closet door and put a hole in it. He said he was leaving, and I told him to go ahead. He proceeded to get his luggage and leave. I got in the car and took a ride. I remember driving while I was crying and talking to the Lord about everything going on in my life. The word of God is the comfort that Christians go to when faced with life's challenges. While I was driving, I began to think about God's word.

He reassured me:

"Many are the afflictions of the righteous: but the Lord
delivereth him out of them all."
Psalms 34:19 (KJV).

When I got back home, Eric had his luggage in the living room ready to go, so I thought. Instead, he asked me if I would come into the bedroom so that we could talk away from the children, and I did. He began to tell me that he was sorry for his actions and that he made a promise to himself never to hit a woman, which is why he hit the closet. He had been exposed to that type of behavior from the men in his family.

24

I also apologized, so we kissed and talked some more, then I volunteered to help him unpack the luggage and put his clothes back in the bedroom. Then, the funniest thing happened, he said, "There are no clothes in the luggage; I was never going anywhere." We laugh about that day even now and thank God for maturity.

I was gaining weight, and I could see it; I would tell myself I was going on a diet. I would try it for a while, but right back into those bad eating habits, I would go. I also believe I am what you would call an emotional eater, and when I would have stress in my life, I would eat comfort food such as fries, chips, cookies, ice cream, butter pecan is my favorite.

These types of food were really causing me to feel even worse, and my breathing wasn't getting better. I could feel the swelling in my feet and legs. This was the point in my life where I had to really press into the Lord because my Dad had gotten worse even with dialysis.

CHAPTER 9

Heartaches and Pain|

June 18th of 2002 is a day I shall never forget. I was at work, and I got a phone call from my mother. I could tell in her voice something was wrong. She asked me if I was sitting down, and I said, "yes." The next words out of her mouth would hurt my heart terribly; she told me that my dad had passed.

This is so hard to write even now; I'm crying tears. The pain of never hearing his voice again, never being able to travel with him to do revivals again, no more vacations, no more of him sneaking money to me, it's funny how he knew when I needed some extra cash. When I called Eric, I was crying uncontrollably. He tried to calm me down, but he decided to pick me up and take me to the hospital when he could.

Have you ever had a situation happen in your life, and you can remember every detail about it? Well, I can remember the very song playing on the radio as we drove to the hospital; it was such a sad day in our family.

My sister Betty was the strong one because she took charge and made the arrangements, she would have her moments of breakdown, but she got it done. Everyone was concerned about me because I was already sick, and the heart-wrenching pain of this loss was not helping. They suggested that I not go to view my dad's body, but I went anyway; what a mistake that was. As soon as we got out of the car to go into the funeral home, I started vomiting. I was so sick and crying uncontrollably. It was just too overwhelming for me.

I was trying to be strong for my mother, but I couldn't. I loved my dad so much we had such a special bond. I was his Trela. What was I going to do without him in my life? People came from all over to his homegoing service. He touched many lives on the battlefield for the Lord, Cuthbert. Sylvester, Camilla, Dawson, Americus, Moultrie in Georgia; Ocala Orlando, Tampa, and St. Petersburg in Florida. Dad went wherever the Lord called him, and on that day, He called him home. He will forever be remembered.

As we returned to my mom's home, we hugged her and told her we would be there for her and that God would see her through this. One thing about death is true — after the friends, the long-distance family, and loved ones leave, that's when it really hits home that the person is never to return, and the loneliness sets in. Honestly, to me, this is when people need to hear from friends and love ones. I'm so glad that God's Word is always there to lean on.

He encourages us through His Word:
"The LORD is nigh unto them that are of a broken heart, and saveth such as be of a contrite spirit."
Psalm 34:18 (KJV).

We all went back to our regular, scheduled lives missing our dad and husband. Life wouldn't be the same, but we persevered with the help of the Lord. My mom began running the ministry, and God truly shined his light on the work she was doing for the kingdom of God. Our family was there for whatever she needed from us. She asked my husband and me to be Co-Pastors of the ministry, and we were honored to do so. I was still suffering from heart problems but doing the Lord's work was most important.

Going back and forth into the hospital had become a routine for me, but one time when I was in the hospital, I became dizzy. I held my head back to see if that would help and when I opened my eyes, four nurses were standing in my room. They asked me if I was ok because I was experiencing irregular heart rhythms. I didn't quite understand what was going on, so I became afraid. The doctor said I needed to be transported to Saint Joseph's Hospital to undergo testing for an ICD (Implantable Cardioverter Defibrillator) to be surgically implanted in my chest to help with the irregular heartbeats. When I received this news, I was by myself, but our spiritual daughter Angela Carr came through the door shortly afterward. She was such a blessing to me at that moment. She assured me that all would be well and as she is known for being a demon slayer, she immediately started talking to the enemy, telling him that he gets NO VICTORY here.

I called my family and told them what the doctor said, and they came to the hospital to see me off. I remember this day so well. The EMTs loaded me up, I said my goodbyes, and my husband said he remembers them wheeling me down the hall to the ambulance. I didn't know that riding in ambulances would become another routine of mine.

My family came to see me the next day. The doctors had already started doing their testing on my heart, which showed that I was having heart arrhythmias that were becoming serious, so the doctor said I needed an Implantable Cardioverter Defibrillator. An ICD is used for heart-failure treatment when the person is at a high risk of dying from an abnormal heart rhythm -- called sudden cardiac death. It is a small device that is implanted in the chest and continually monitors the heart's rhythm.

I'm thankful for having a relationship with our Heavenly Father because His word is in me, and it gives me the strength that I need. My nurse came in to talk with me about the defibrillator. She asked me if I was afraid, and I said, "yes." I was crying because, in my mind, all I could envision at that time was my life being over. When I tell you, trials help to refine us, yes, they do. I didn't realize at the time that the Lord was developing the spirit of an intercessor in me. Learning to pray became natural to me during my health crisis; I felt so much better about my condition and life after praying. An intercessor is a person who prays for others. They have built up a prayer regime that allows them to believe God can and will do anything for anybody.

One day I was praying, and the Lord reminded me of how a football player runs in and intercepts a ball. He gains control of the ball for his team. Although not quite the same as interceptors, intercessors pray on behalf of others, and in doing so, those prayers do indeed intercept what the enemy is trying to do. Prayer is a powerful weapon that I use daily, and my prayer life went to another level when I was diagnosed with heart disease.

"Fear thou not; for I am with thee: be not dismayed;
for I am thy God: I will strengthen thee;
yea, I will help thee; yea, I will uphold thee with
the right hand of my righteousness."
Isaiah 41:10

After reading this word and talking with my family, I knew God would take care of me, and I decided to have the procedure done.

I remember the surgeon trying to push the device in my chest area but having trouble, they did not give me enough anesthesia because I moaned, and he said, "ok, I'm sorry, I'll stop." When I got back to my room and was awake, the doctor came in. He said he had trouble getting one of the wires where it needed to go, and we would go with what he did and "see how it goes." My husband and mother took me home.

I stayed at my mother's home for about two weeks to heal. My sister Sangra and her family had just moved from Atlanta and stayed at Mom's until they found a house, so she was my nurse, doctor, friend, enemy, mother, nutritionist, and then some. When I went back home, I-decided to quit my job. I was the daycare director for nine years, and I so enjoyed my job. When I told my staff I was leaving, they were so hurt and saddened. I must say, I cared greatly for the women who made up my staff. At one point, I managed 26 ladies who were genuine and kind to the children and the parents. After getting out of the hospital, my cardiologist suggested that I apply for disability, so I did.

CHAPTER 10

The Disability Journey Begins

After being denied twice, I decided to get myself a lawyer. The Firm Wilson and Berry came aboard and helped me gather things together for court. During this time, it seemed as if I would never get approved. In the meantime, our bills were piling up due to us only having one income; however, this is where I get to brag on our God. When I tell people this testimony, it is hard for them to believe, but it's true. Our rent got behind by $5000, and we weren't put out, nor were we harassed about when we would pay it. We talked to our landlord and explained that I was without a job due to heart failure and had applied for disability. We intended to pay her whatever we owed her. She said she would wait for us to give her the money, but she also asked us not to leave her without all the unpaid back rent. We told her that God would not bless us if we did that.

Let me say this; it goes back to being good stewards over what God has given you. If you want to be blessed, you have got to be obedient to the word of the Lord and give your tithe. Life continued to be a struggle, but the Lord saw us through. One time, we were blessed with a lump sum of money right at the needed time, and we were able to pay our landlord what we owed her.

I will never forget the tears she shed. She told us she didn't want to harass us, but there was a concern about whether we would pay her because some previous tenants had stiffed her, and she didn't want that to happen again. Our relationship with her grew to be incredibly special from that point on. She said we were Christian people with whom she takes pleasure in having as tenants.

I believe in keeping my house clean and neat, and every time she would come over for inspections, she would tell me how happy she was that I keep a clean and tidy home. I was raised by a mother who did not play about keeping her house clean. She would teach us all about being clean and not living in a nasty home. We've lived in the same place for 20 years, even though our landlord has passed on.

My disability was approved after a while, and I gave God all the glory. When I stood before the judge, and he found out that my heart ejection fraction was only beating twenty percent, he was upset that I wasn't approved for disability earlier. "Considering the factors," the judge said to my lawyer, "I will award her full approval." That day, as I walked out with my lawyer, he said, "you will be receiving your letter shortly, along with your benefits."

I got in my truck and cried, thanking the Lord all the way home, excited to share with my husband. We paid our tithe so that the Lord would continue to bless us. I purchased a Chrysler Town and Country Van with all the amenities, and my husband was also blessed with a brand-new Chevy Silverado.

I know what He's done for me.

Our children were coming of age, and life was moving right along; the church was growing, new members were being added to the church daily, such as should be saved. My mom started a church fellowship and named it, *The 5th Sunday Gathering* with other pastors and their congregation: Pastor Westbrook, Bishop Mobley, Apostle & Co-Pastor Chambers, Pastor Carroll, Apostle Carr, Apostle Mccoy. Her vision for our *5th Sunday Fellowship Services* was to gather at one another's church.

The Lord was blessing the ministry with new members. When hurricane Katrina hit New Orleans in 2005, some victims evacuated to Albany, Georgia, and joined the church. We were preparing for my mom's anniversary celebration. A new member, Evangelist Dorothea Royster, asked if the church would allow her old pastor from New Orleans to give the Sunday message. Of course, everyone agreed, so she invited the church, *House of Deliverance*, and their Pastor Apostle Mary Trask.

Our spiritual daughter, Sister Melody Peterson (Melp as we call her), came into our lives through this service. She was the pastor's adjutant. To make a long story short, our lives came together with purpose. She would eventually become such a great blessing to my family and me. She would come to visit, go to church with us, help me around the house, just anything I needed her to do. She was a willing vessel. I'm so grateful to the Lord for allowing our paths to cross. When they call her to tell her I'm sick, here she comes. It would bother me how she would travel dark country roads, as she refers to them, to come to see about me.

The children absolutely adore her, and the thing about this entire relationship is that Sister Melody or Melp is older than I am but gives my husband and me the utmost respect. She says we are her spiritual parents because we have helped her grow in many areas in her life, for which God gets all the credit. She and I would keep in touch, and it so happened; one Sunday, I was on my way over to my mom's house, and I was talking with her when I was hit on the driver's side by a Ford Explorer. There were three teenagers in the truck driving fast, trying to get to the movie theater because they were late. I had glass in my hair, the left side of my neck was cut up, I had a broken rib. It wasn't good. — BUT GOD. I was in the hospital for about a week. When I came home, we filed a lawsuit.

My dear friend, Melp, was right there for me. She came from Louisiana to help take care of me, oh how I thank the Lord for placing her in our lives. It took about a year and a half before the lawsuit was settled; the Lord sent it right on time.

The Lord was blessing me in many ways, but then sickness came into the picture. I had to be admitted into the hospital because so much fluid had built up around my heart. It was so hard for me to breathe again. I was also having trouble with my stomach, and my doctor decided I needed to have a gastroenterologist see what was going on. After the procedure, they tried to wake me from the anesthesia, and I went into cardiac arrest. I remember the nurse saying, "Mrs. Taylor, Mrs. Taylor!" I heard her calling for the doctor, and she said, "Mrs. Taylor, I'm sorry, but we've got to shock you." The next thing I remember is being in ICU. My husband began to tell me I'd been in the hospital for a week on a ventilator, and he suggested that the doctors refer me to Emory.

So, I was transported by ambulance to Emory. The doctors began running test after test, doing blood work checking to see just how weak my heart was. My mom was with me during this time until my husband could tie up loose ends at home. I couldn't wait to see him. I remember Dr. Book having to go through the right side of my neck to do a right side of the heart catheterization to check my heart pressures. This was when I remember being completely still because I did *not* want to get shocked.

CHAPTER 11

The Famous LVAD

They decided to move me to a regular room to watch me and see how I would progress. My mom and husband would sit with me day in and day out, reading scriptures and encouraging me to hang on in there.

I remember my mom going to a revival in Sylvester, Ga, where she met a Co-Pastor who gave her testimony about her heart condition and how God had healed her; my mom couldn't wait to come and tell me. So, I went with her the next night and met Pastor Tronda Westbrook, who became a spiritual blessing in my life.

When I first got sick and was placed in the hospital, I told my mom to call her and ask her to pray for me, and she did. I love to hear her say, "To God Be the Glory." It's like I know God is in control when she says those words.

One time I looked up, and she had come to visit me in Atlanta, I tell you I love this woman of Faith, if you are down, just listening to her tell her testimony of how sick her heart was — But God; and I knew if God healed her heart, He could heal mine as well. She and I don't talk daily, but we keep in touch with one another and always share the good news of Jesus Christ.

There were many days of longing to be home with my family instead of lying in the hospital bed. It was so hard to handle the loneliness. One day, I had gotten up to walk around the unit, and when I got back to my room, I started feeling funny, but I didn't say anything. Eric hadn't eaten yet, so I told him to go and get himself something to eat. He said, "no, I'm going to stay here because you don't look right. Then the next thing I remember is I became short of breath. I was gasping for air, saying, "I can't breathe, I can't breathe. The nurses came running! They told me to lie back in the bed, and then they called for the resident to come, who immediately told the nurses, "get the crash cart!"

Then, I coded. Eric told me that I coded for about ten minutes. I remember a doctor got on top of my chest, performing CPR. He was pushing my chest in as hard as he could, trying to get a pulse. I could hear them saying, "stay with us, Mrs. Taylor."

One of the nurses said, "if you can hear me squeeze my hand," and I squeezed her hand. Eric was to the side praying with a nurse. He said that there were about twenty people in that room when he opened his eyes, and they were all working to save my life.

I know what He's done for me.

My chest was so sore by the time they rushed me to CCU. They had placed a balloon pump in my left groin to help my heart pump more blood, but they had just taken it out because I was doing better. It had to be put back in. Dr. Jokhadar, one of the cardiologists who specialized in advanced heart failure, came in and said, "Mrs. Taylor, I'm sorry, but I've got to shock you to get your heart back in rhythm." After that, he proceeded to put the balloon pump back in. I stayed in CCU for a while, but the heart was not getting any better.

The doctors were trying their best to get my heart to stay in rhythm, but it was just too weak, so the LVAD team came and began talking with my family and me about having surgery done on my heart. An LVAD is a left ventricular device used for assisting in cardiac circulation. It helps pump the oxygenated blood to your heart. They showed us a film about what to expect while living with the device. Patients who had already had the surgery were telling their stories in the film. I was so overwhelmed that I cried. The LVAD coordinator, Corby, assured me that I would be glad I had it after I had the surgery and began to feel better.

At that time, the enemy tried to tell me I wouldn't enjoy life anymore. The one thing I couldn't do anymore that really hurt was I wouldn't be able to swim, and our family loves the water. Nonetheless, I talked it over and over with my husband and mother. They convinced me that the benefits of having it outweighed the negative, so I decided to have the surgery.

My surgeon, Dr. Vega, introduced himself to us and asked us if we had any questions concerning the surgery. Of course, we did, so he answered them all and assured us that he had done a number of these surgeries. The doctor then told us what to expect afterward. He said the surgery would take place that Tuesday. It was Sunday evening February, 7, the same night the New Orleans Saints won the Super Bowl.

We contacted our family, gave them the information about the surgery, and asked them to pray.

Our spiritual daughter, Melp, made her way to Atlanta to be there for the surgery. That Tuesday morning, I had LVAD surgery. I was so scared, but I prayed and asked the Lord to please help me through the surgery. I remember them taking me into the operating room full of machines, technicians, nurses, and doctors. One of the nurses said, "Mrs. Taylor, we're going to put you on top of this table and get you set up for the surgery." Then they put an oxygen mask over my mouth and told me to breathe in and count to three. I only remember counting to two.

Chapter 12

The Attachment

The next thing I recall was opening my eyes to a small room with a nurse standing over me, checking my vital signs. I tried to move and realized I couldn't. They had me strapped to the bed because the LVAD was attached to me. I didn't know you can't get up without having the bag. The bag contains the LVAD device that pumps the blood through the heart. That was my trial of having a bag attached to me 24 hours a day, seven days a week. I really couldn't comprehend the LVAD being with me everywhere I went. When it was first explained to my husband and me, I didn't have *this* picture in mind, but it came to life when I tried to get out of bed for the first time.

The physical therapist was there to help me try to stand, but I couldn't; my legs were very weak. I had been in the hospital for over a month on my back. I had lost a great deal of weight, too. She helped me to stand while I was holding on under her arms. Although I did get up and stand briefly, it felt like I had run a country mile. I was so fatigued, but she continued to come back and work with me on getting out of bed. She consistently reminded me ALWAYS to grab my bag, which was attached to my right side with two titanium batteries inside of it.

During this period, I remember our spiritual daughter being in the room while I slept, and I could hear her speaking in her heavenly language, declaring and decreeing that I shall live and not die. I also remember seeing my brother, Woodall, and my mom come in for a visit. He told me, "Tre, you look good." That made me feel better.

I was in ICU when I got my LVAD on Feb 9th, 2010. I spent my 44th birthday looking out the window to see that it had snowed in Atlanta. My Aunt Nella Wise had sent me an edible arrangement that I couldn't have. Patients cannot have arrangements in ICU, so I gave it to the nurse's station; they all came in to say thanks.

After making progress, they moved me to a regular floor, the 4th floor, which I had already been on so many times before. The nurses knew me, and they were excited about the success of the surgery.

My family could come and visit me since I was no longer in ICU. Tan, Jean, Betty, my aunt Sharon, and my cousins were excited to see me, and it gave me such joy to see them.

My husband had taken leave from his job to stay with me during my recovery. He was such a blessing. He had to deal with me always being hot and wanting the air on, and he was a trooper. We often talk about how he would ask the nurses for more blankets to cover his head because I always felt hot, and now, I walk around with socks and a blanket because I'm always cold. His commitment to me and our marriage takes me back to that three-strand cord; together is always better, team Taylor.

I had physical therapy coming in every day to work with me on getting back to normal. The LVAD was my "new normal." Emory has a team of LVAD techs, Kevin, and Neal who would come and monitor the machine, watching the machine's speed. There was so much traffic in and out of my room, with everyone trying to get me better. I will recommend Emory Hospital to anyone requiring medical attention. While I was there, I felt like I was the only patient of importance.

Eric was right there asking the nurses questions about what he could do to help. My mom would come back and forth, praying over me and reading scriptures to me. She made sure that the word of God was planted on the inside.

She would always read Psalm 118:17:

"I shall not die, but live,
and declare the works of the Lord." (KJV)

I would try not to get depressed, but it was hard; life as I knew it was no more. Walking around with the LVAD battery pack attached to me and unsure what to expect, thoughts of death would come into my mind. I had to fight like a warrior and tell the enemy I would not give up. My husband told me, "Baby, we are going to get through this." He said he would be with me along this journey, and he has — every step of the way, crying in secret, worrying, and praying yet trusting that all would be well.

CHAPTER 13

The New Normal

My LVAD coordinator, Corby, was a great inspiration in my life as well because she was always and still is there to be of assistance in any way she can. As I continued to get better, she would come by and keep me encouraged about how much progress I was making with coming familiar with handling the bag. I was concerned about the bag being attached and taking care of the site where they had surgically placed the cord that attached to the machine. I could not leave the hospital until Eric passed the test on properly dressing an LVAD site. When I first got the VAD, my husband was taught the importance of ensuring the procedure was done twice a day. He was so afraid of messing up because he loves me so much and didn't want to hurt me. He had to suit up in a surgical gown and gloves, everything must be sterile, and everyone in the room had to wear masks to keep down germs. He told me afterward, "Baby, I was so hot in all that stuff, and I was sweating profusely."

He passed the test! Praise the Lord! Then it was my turn to learn how to properly take my batteries apart and replace them with another pair. They lasted about sixteen hours, but you never want to leave them in that long. I was nervous doing this part, trying to remember the different sounds it makes to alarm you when something goes wrong with the machine. Even now, I'm just thanking God because that day was hard for me, knowing that I was holding my lifeline in my hand.

I know what He's done for me.

Eric and the LVAD tech, Kevin, and I went for a drive in the truck to see how I would do my first time out of the hospital. It was scary, but I did it. The therapist took me for a walk down the hall to get adjusted to walking with an LVAD. She watched as I detached from the cable that was hooked into the wall and connected my batteries to the machine inside the bag. I then walked as my mom and husband watched and encouraged me by saying, "yeah, girl, you got it!" I was so proud of myself at that moment.

The therapist said, "You did such a good job; let's go see some of your nurses in ICU and show them you are up and walking. I'll wheel you in the chair to the unit because I know that walk will be too much for you to do." As I entered ICU, the nurses remembered me and smiled and congratulated me, telling me how good I looked. They encouraged me by telling me that I would one day come back and be walking and feeling better because of what the LVAD offers its recipients, a better life.

Dr. Vega came in and asked if I was ready to go home. "Yes!" It had been so long since I'd seen my children and my family. He told me that the LVAD coordinator would come with all my equipment to take home with me, and afterward, he would discharge me. My heart was incredibly happy.

Corby came in and brought a new coordinator with her named Kris Wittersheim. Little did I know that this God-given Angel would play such a tremendous role in my life. The two of them started going over all the items I had to take home with me. Then, Kevin, the LVAD tech, came to go over everything about the machine one more time. That was a stressful day; nonetheless, I was excited to be going home. After about 4 hours, Dr. Vega finally came and said, "you are free to go."

It was about 7:00 pm that evening when my mom, Eric, and I traveled home. Eric was pulled over that night because one of his headlights was out. He told the officer, "Sir, could you please hurry? We are on our way home from the hospital, and I know my wife is tired. It's been a long trip." Oh, happy day. We drove up to the house, and I immediately started crying and thanking the Lord for being able to return to my home. My children were so excited to see me but scared to touch me. I assured them it was ok to touch me carefully. It was the start of a new journey for all of us.

Our daughter Kristen and her dear friend LaTandria took care of our youngest son, Joshua, and TJ. They were the parents while their dad and I were away. LaTandria was a good cook and a helpful friend to Kristen and our family. Her thoughtfulness and generosity will always be gratefully remembered.

That night she soaked my feet in some Epsom salt and water to help with the swelling. As she was rubbing my feet, she said, "Pastor Taylor, I can hear a humming coming from your stomach." I told her and the children that it was the LVAD machine running, and they must help me keep the batteries charged. That was a teachable moment about the LVAD and how it operates. The first time I experienced my defibrillator charging up was when my Aunt Nella was lying in bed with me talking, and I heard it getting ready to fire. Lord, I was terrified. Boom,

Boom, Boom, that was the sound of the defibrillator going off, then it stopped. She called for Eric to come because I was getting shocked. He called the doctor on call, Dr. Smith, who said I should transmit the information from the ICD (Implanted Cardioverter Defibrillator) to them. I had to transmit every week to the Boston Scientific company to check the life of the defibrillator's battery. After Dr. Smith received the results, he called and told me to see my local cardiologist, Dr. Craig Mitchell, the next morning, and I did. I was told that if it were not for the LVAD, I would have died, the Physician's Assistant showed me how my heart had gotten out of rhythm, and the LVAD kept pumping blood.

I know what He's done for me.

At that point, I thought about how I didn't want to have the surgery, but that day, I was so glad I did. I was still weak and unable to walk a lot, but I persevered. It was a struggle remembering to grab my bag when I got up. I also had to begin taking coumadin, a blood thinner, to keep the blood thin while circulating through the machine. The thing about coumadin is you must be aware of the greens you are consuming. Certain green vegetables or too much of others can lower and raise the levels in your blood, which is why I would have to stay in contact with the coumadin clinic. I would have my blood drawn at the local lab, and they would call me with instructions. Sometimes I had to take shots (Lovenox) in my stomach if my levels were off to prevent the blood clots.

CHAPTER 14

Tried and Tested, Tested and Tried

The church and my family were so excited that I was home and doing better; they had an appreciation service for me. Pastors with whom we affiliate were part of it, Co-Pastor Chambers, Apostle, Prophetess Tyson, The Westbrook's, Pastor Carroll, Bishop Mobley, friends, and loved ones from all around came to thank God for sparing my life. I cried through the entire service; I was so overwhelmed with gratitude for all the love shown to my family and me. God has been so good to me even in the midst of all that I had already endured. The Lord was steadily showing me that He has my life in His hands.

Attending church was something I was excited to start doing again. Even though I got shocked at the back of the church, I kept going. I would have to go back and forth to my local cardiologist to keep checking on the defibrillator to ensure that I was doing well. As time went on, I had some good days, but I would continue to get shocked. I preached, and after I got home and started cooking, I got shocked. I was sitting at home in my chair and got shocked. Emory decided that I needed to have another wire attached to my defibrillator because I was not getting enough electricity to get my heart back in rhythm.

So, off to the hospital, I went. Eric and Mom went with me. We stayed in a hotel in Atlanta the night before the procedure to get a good night's rest. All went well, and I came home with my life-saving equipment reinforced to help my failing heart.

There were times when I would get up and forget I was attached to a bag that had to travel with me everywhere I would go.

The funny thing about this LVAD was when they gave me the bag, it looked like a cross-body bag, and quite a few people would mistake it for my handbag, but it was not. One day I had gone to the mall to shop at Lane Bryant for a new bra; I had lost so much weight I was in a different size. The associate told me, ma'am, you can put your purse down, and we will size you. I started smiling and told her, no, I can't put this down; this is my lifeline.

People would ask me why I always had the bag with me. Explaining the LVAD was something I had to get adjusted to because it was a new procedure that people were not aware of. Former Vice President, Dick Cheney, was the first person I know of who had an LVAD. As I was getting adjusted to having the Vad, I preached more and went to places more, just living life and maintaining.

Then sickness hit again, but this time it was my mom. She found out she had breast cancer. We took her to Atlanta to an oncologist who performed surgery and had her ready to come home the next day. She was such a trooper too. She continued to trust in the Lord and believe that He would see her through and that He did. My mom didn't have to undergo any radiation nor chemotherapy.

I know what He's done for me.

Sparing my mother's life was nothing short of a miracle, and who wouldn't serve a God like this.

The Bible declares:

"So shall they fear the name of the Lord from the west, and his glory from the rising of the sun. When the enemy shall come in like a flood, the Spirit of the Lord shall lift a standard against him".
Isaiah 59:19.

When I feel like I've been singled out, I reach within and remember my God-given power and strength, along with His Word, to affirm that.

"So shall they fear the name of the Lord from the west and his glory from the rising of the sun."
Isaiah 59:19 (KJV)

My mom's recovery went well, and she returned to preaching the gospel. Although she gave up pastoring the church, she continues to minister the word of the Lord.

It was hard for my family to find another ministry because that was the only church I'd been a part of. So Eric and I prayed and kept seeking the Lord. We believe in allowing God to plant you in a church ministry, and if He plants you there, you will grow right there.

One day, when my hairstylist, Samantha Jackson, and I were talking about our husbands, I realized that our husbands needed to meet because they seem to have so many things in common. She asked me to come to the grand opening of the church she and her husband were opening, Kingdom Life Ministries. So my family and I went. It was such a powerful service! The children enjoyed it, too, which was a blessing to my husband and me. So, we decided to go back to their bible study, and we enjoyed that as well.

His Word affirms that the Lord is in control of our lives:

> *"For I know the thoughts that I think toward you, saith the*
> *LORD, thoughts of peace, and not of evil, to give you an*
> *expected end."*
> Jeremiah 29:11 (KJV).

Eric and I continued to pray and seek the Lord about that church. We decided not to go from church to church, so we just fellowshipped with them since everyone liked that church. The people of the church congregation were so warm and showed us so much love. The pastor, Rodney Jackson, gave us a chance to have words if we wanted. He has such a caring and loving spirit. I believe that the congregation will have some of the same characteristics as the pastor.

I had never been in any other church for years. It was hard transitioning, but my family was ready to join the ministry, so we did. We had three children at home during this time, Kristen, Bethany, and Josh. Serving in ministry was extremely important to us, so we all went to work. Eric and I were ordained as associate pastors, Bethany and Kristen joined the praise team, and Joshua was a junior usher. My LVAD was allowing me to do wonderful things in the ministry and with my family. I was able to go to Virginia with my husband to his sister's wedding, and we had such a great time.

I went on several mother-daughter trips to Florida and Augusta, Georgia. I enjoyed some good times and had good days for a while, but then it seemed as though I had to go into the hospital every time I would return from a trip. My device would fire, and I would have to call the ambulance. The LVAD was doing what it's supposed to do, but my heart was continuing to fail. I went to the hospital so many times that I stopped counting after ten.

One time, when I went to the hospital, it was late at-night when the transport team got there to take me to Emory. It was cold, and the ambulance had to stop in Macon, Georgia, to switch out drivers, so I had to be taken out of one truck and put in another. I remember saying to myself, "Lord, please fix it for me."

CHAPTER 15

The Struggle was Real

One afternoon, as I was on my way to Emory, the driver had to pull over and call for another ambulance to come and get me because they started having trouble with that one. As my mother was on her way up shortly after that, she said they passed us beside the road. She told our spiritual daughter, Melp, "that's my daughter in that truck." I was on the side of the road for quite some time BUT GOD. That LVAD continued to pump the blood, and I continued to ask the Lord to spare my life.

When we got to Emory, there were doctors and nurses everywhere waiting on me. They started hooking me up to all types of machines, especially the crash cart, which had become very familiar to me. Once again, the Lord had my life which has consisted of many twists and turns and just as many ups and downs. However, I'm still here to tell the story.

The Word of God declares:

"These things I have spoken unto you, that in me ye might have peace. In the world ye shall have tribulation: but be of good cheer; I have overcome the world."
John 16:33 (KJV)

You've got to learn to love the struggle. There have been many days wherein I wanted to give up on life, but the call of God upon my life caused me to gain an even greater strength that I didn't even realize I possessed. Going through trials will prove to you and show you what you're really made of and made for.

God's Word states:

"Therefore, I take pleasure in infirmities, in reproaches,
in necessities, in persecutions, in distresses for Christ's
sake: for when I am weak, then am I strong."
2 Corinthians 12:10 KJV

April 2, 2019, started with me doing my morning *Pausing for Prayer* Facebook live broadcast. After the broadcast, my husband, our son, and I left to attend court for Joshua. Not knowing what to expect, we made our way to the magistrate court. As we arrived and entered, people of all types began to appear for court to answer the charge placed upon them.

Joshua was arrested on February 10, 2019. After his dad picked him up from work that night around 12, his dad came into the house, but Joshua did not. So, I asked my husband, "Hunny, where is Joshua?"

Eric replied, "Tre when I drove up outside, there was a car waiting for Joshua. I told him, 'Son, you need to come on in the house.'"

I remember that night so well because the Lord spoke a word into my spirit concerning the world.

He said that trouble is always waiting on you to say yes and dive into it. Well, Joshua didn't come right in, so I texted him a message that stated, "come in NOW!! I emphasize the NOW in capital letters because my spirit felt the urgency for him to come on in because trouble was waiting on him. He didn't come in.

My husband and I went on to bed. At about 3:30 am, a knock came at the door. It was the mother of the driver who Joshua left the house with, informing us that the sheriff had arrested Joshua, and the other two people in the car, were not charged.

This is a teachable moment for everyone reading this book. Please tell these children who are brought up in a bible-based home, with tongue-speaking parents, and saved grandparents, that things will not go easy for them. Far too many prayers go up for them that they will surrender to the will of the Lord for their lives.

As we sat there, Joshua, Eric, and I with our pastor Rodney Jackson, it was evident that Joshua was scared. I could see the sadness on his face. After a recess, the judge proceeded with the sentencing of the day. He eventually called Joshua's name. The judge placed Joshua on probation. God had proven himself to be faithful and allowed him to get himself together, but he continued to spiral out of control.

On July 18, Joshua was put in jail. Although having a child in jail is hard, God is still good. Emotions running high, I waivered between wanting to cry and being strong, then the frustration set in because Joshua didn't have to do what he did.

I still wasn't feeling like my old self, but I trusted God to touch my body with His healing hands and give me a miraculous testimony.

I've been through so much. I've thought about my ministry on Facebook, *Pausing for Prayer,* and how I should go about moving forward because even when adversities happen, we still must press on. My son pushes me to THE SON.

My prayer during this time was and still is, "God, I know you are still in charge of my life and Joshua's life.

Please keep him safe and do a great work in him."

On August 6, 2019, I had a doctor's appointment in Atlanta at Emory, and Joshua had to appear in court as well. I waited all day to hear from my husband about what happened. When he called me, he said that Joshua was given 252 days in jail for a probation violation. Lord, my child. A mother never wants to have to deal with seeing their child locked up, so I feel for him. But then again, Joshua was warned so many times about the life he was living. My greatest prayer is that he surrenders to the will of the Lord for his life.

My emotions got the best of me, especially since I wasn't feeling my best. Jesus, I need you.

CHAPTER 16

Getting Listed for Transplant

It was about 4:30 in the morning on August 19, and I couldn't sleep. I was asking God to heal this body of mine as I laid awake while experiencing some pain. I believe God can do anything but fail.

Sometimes the enemy brings thoughts to mind like: we will never be happy, never get out of debt, and never have or be better. When those thoughts come to mind, I really try to lean on the promises of God.

August is the eighth month, and the number eight in the Bible represents new beginnings. I was anxious to see what new thing the Lord would do for the Taylors.

Inventory time…

I was released from the hospital; Joshua was in jail, and Eric lost his job.

"In all my trials, Lord, you've pulled me through, and I must trust that EVERYTHING is going to be alright."

I wrote in my journal, "I'm laying here once again at 10:52 pm. I'm sleepy, but I can't go to sleep so, I'm writing what's on my mind.

"We must go to Joshua's committal hearing in the morning. He called us tonight and seemed to be in good spirits. I'm so thankful for the change that God is doing in him. My prayer is that this will not be jailhouse religion but a real relationship with Christ. He owes Him his life because God has been good to Joshua."

The next day, August 20, 2019, was the day Joshua went to court for the crime of burglary. We got there at 8:30 and stayed until 10:30 because we found out that his committal hearing was not on the docket until 1:00. We got back about 12:20 and stayed until the very end, which was about 4:00, only to find out that the judge didn't rule or anything because Joshua must serve his 252-day sentence first.

I hadn't seen him since he left the house on July 18, and I was glad to see him that day. I know someone was praying for me because I didn't cry when I saw him; my heart was filled with joy to know that my son was alive and well. Some mothers will never see their sons again, but God is so faithful. Joshua being locked up really got to me some days. We weren't financially able to keep money on his books, so he often wasn't able to call home. I missed the sound of his voice. It's funny how the Lord prepared me for Joshua being gone because there were many days Joshua wasn't home. He would leave and stay gone for days and weekends. I miss seeing him. He doesn't want me to visit him at the jail, and I'm okay with that. Hearing the sound of his voice would reassure me that he was okay. I can discern, by hearing his voice, how he's doing. Joshua always tells me to keep my head up and that he's keeping his head up, too.

I wrote in my journal, "I'm truly thankful for what God is doing in his life. I'm believing God for Joshua to be a mighty man of God when he does get out."

On August 29, my Emory doctor, Dr. Gupta, talked with me about being put on the heart transplant list. She told me that the team had been discussing my case. Because I had significant weight loss, they want to push for it. The paperwork was filed with my insurance company. I wrote, "All I know is—God knows everything. My life is in His hands. There is so much going on in my life right now. I'm just seeking God and trying to listen and be obedient to what He's saying. I can't sleep, I'm hurting, and I'm emotional."

This struggle was real, so I would pray, " Lord, please help me. I don't want to go back to the hospital, touch and heal this site that's paining me because I know you are able. Please remove all this bloating in my stomach."

Despite the praying, I still went back to the hospital on September 5. I was hurting so badly and feeling awful. I prayed, "Lord, please show them what to do; you're the great Physician you made this body. They don't want to take me off the sotalol, the medication helping to keep my heartbeat regulated, because it's doing what they want it to do.

Loresa, the spiritual counselor at Emory, prayed with us and touched and agreed that the doctors would find out what's making me feel so fatigued and sick. About three hours later, Dr. Smith came back around to tell us that they would take me off two of my medicines.

God is Faithful. Lord, these are some things I desire to do:
- Go to Baton Rouge, Louisiana, for the service at SBN
- Go to Mattson, Illinois, for a service with the Ray sisters
- Take my grandchildren on a nice vacation
- Take Taylor and me on a nice vacation.
- I desire to bless my mother financially.
- Give my testimony on live tv.

Take Jesus with you through your stuff.

I came home from the hospital on Thursday, September 19. I was feeling weak but pressing my way anyhow. In the middle of the night, Melp had come to help me. She is such a gift to the body of Christ and the Taylor family. I ask the Lord to bless her as he knows what's best for her.

While I was in the hospital, I had a colonoscopy done. Omg, I tell you—that was no fun. They started the process for me to get listed for transplant. Eric and I, along with Melp, filled out all my paperwork for my heart transplant surgery. There was a plethora of paperwork to be done and turned back in before having the surgery. They tell you all the negative things that can happen, but I chose to believe that God would give me a miracle. Why would He bring me to this point to leave me?

Sometimes the enemy would tell me to "just give up," but there was something (The Holy Spirit) on the inside that kept pushing me. There was so much going on. My husband still didn't have a job, Joshua was still in jail, needing money weekly, and we wanted to move closer to Atlanta. Whew! Without God, I would be drifting aimlessly, like a ship without a sail.

The Word of God declares that if your strength is small, you will faint in the day of adversity. "I want to hang on in here, BUT, PLEASE, LORD, touch this body and strengthen me in the name of Jesus.

Lord, I need a financial miracle! This trial is so hard, and I pray I don't fail."

The Bible says,
"God has not given us a spirit of fear."
2 Timothy 1:7

I couldn't go to my own bathroom because I dreaded having to feel the fast heart rhythms. "I'm at my wit's end, Lord, you're going to have to move in a mighty way, please, Lord. Lord, please deliver."

As I sat down from using the bathroom, I could feel the shock coming on; BOOM, BOOM, BOOM, and I was off to the hospital again.

That time was vastly different. They placed me in a helicopter because my heart would not get back into rhythm, and they needed to get me to Emory quickly.

CHAPTER 17

A New Heart

After doing extensive blood work, talking with the Heart Transplant team, and bringing my family in for a meeting on October 16 at 9:10 am, I was told they were putting me on the transplant list for a heart. My family had orientation concerning what to expect after the transplant.

During the waiting process, physical therapists would come in and work with me in CCU to try and keep my strength up. The chaplains would talk with me about my beliefs, and my family would come and keep me encouraged. My pastor and his wife came. Elder Fields, the elder in our church, came to visit, and we had a very rewarding conversation.

I was trying to hang in there even though patients were dying all around me. I've come to know that death is a spirit, and if the Lord has not said it is your time, the spirit of death passes you by, and you shall live.

My transplant was done on October 27, 2019, which is also Eric's birthday. My beautiful husband said, "This is the greatest birthday gift I've ever been given." What I remember is waking up in ICU attached to a lot of drains. They had to lift me out of bed using a harness to sit me up. I remember just sitting quietly, trying to take it all in. My chest had many stitches, and there was pain. Physical therapists would help me exercise my feet and try standing. Eventually, after the drainage tubes were removed and I could get up and walk around, I was moved out of ICU to a regular floor on the 4E wing. They were elated to see me because they remember my LVAD journey, and to see me with a new heart was a joy.

I stayed there for about a week, then transferred to Emory's Rehab across the street. Oh my, that's when the true journey began. I must mention that Sister Melody is still with me during this journey.

Rehab started IMMEDIATELY the next morning at 6:00, which is when they begin the day. Breakfast, bath, and then it's time for therapy. I had the opportunity to work with different therapists, who each had their expertise, such as speech, occupational and physical.

During that time, I was very weak, but they showed me no mercy. They were very nice, but they pushed me every day to work hard on getting stronger. While in speech therapy, I would have help with remembering certain things because I lost some oxygen to my brain during surgery, which caused me to have some short-term memory loss. It's truly not a good experience to not remember certain things that you know you should remember, but you can't, such as my husband's birthday, the day I had my transplant.

It would take me some time to remember what certain things were, like an ice cream scoop, animal names, and different people's names. My speech therapist worked with me by showing me pictures that would help jar my memory. She told me to look at it as going a different route to remember. I would know what I was seeing, but I couldn't explain it, so working with pictures helped.

My mom, Eric, Kristen, and Melp were right there with me, encouraging me to give it my all. Eric and Kristen would go back and forth to home, while sister Melp would stay and help me. She would go to the different sessions and report back to my family about my progress. I worked hard, and eventually, it came time for me to go to the Mason house.

Mason House is designed for transplant patients to come and stay while they have appointments at the hospital, like biopsies, bone density scans, and blood work. It was a time of healing for me as well. During my time there, Eric and Kristen stayed with me. They would talk with me and ask me questions concerning my thoughts on everything that had taken place. I would cry a great deal, and I still don't know why, but they were so patient with me.

Eating became a problem for me, everything tasted like lead, and most of the time, I had no appetite, and the weight was coming off. So many nights of insomnia, Eric would read the Bible to me, play inspirational music, but still no sleep. Much of what I was feeling was related to the side effects of all the medicines I was taking—36 pills at one time!

I know what He's done for me.

They tell you in the beginning about certain things to expect, but I was just elated to have a new heart and a chance at a better life. "Well, Mrs. Taylor, it's two days before Thanksgiving 2019. Would you like to go home?" The doctor finally released me to go home, oh happy day!

We traveled about an hour, then I got out and walked around to stretch my legs. Eric had to help me get in and out; I was still weak. As we turned off U.S. Highway 19 onto Endoline drive, I saw my house, tears began to flow, and my hands went up to praise my God for allowing me to make it home one more time. Thank you, Jesus!

The house looked like new money to me; Kristen had bought me a new recliner to rest in because I couldn't lift my legs high enough to get in our bed. Our Thanksgiving was free from noise because I had to be cautious about being around people. My immune system could easily be compromised. My mom came over and brought us thanksgiving dinner. She and my uncle Danny were all the visitors for the day.

My appetite still had not returned, I tried eating a little dressing, but that was about it. I continued to rest and get better day by day. Home therapists had started coming and working with me, physical, occupational, and speech.

One day, while doing physical therapy, we noticed a blood clot had formed in my right thigh area. Being on my back in the hospital for such a long time was the cause. It was swollen, but I didn't have any pain; thank the Lord. Emory ordered an ultrasound which showed inside the clot; hence they started me on a blood thinner, Eliquis, to help dissolve it.

Working with therapy really helped me gain my strength back. However, home therapy was just short-term; therefore, I had to begin going to a local facility. On my final day of home therapy, I had to get in the car and drive to ensure that I felt comfortable doing it again. Even though some LVAD patients would drive, I was advised not to drive when I first got it, so I didn't drive. Consequently, my husband Eric and our children had to drive for me.

"Lo, children are a heritage of the Lord: and the fruit
of the womb is his reward. As arrows are in the hand
of a mighty man, so are children of the youth.
Happy is the man that hath his quiver full of
them: they shall not be ashamed, but they shall
speak with the enemies in the gate."
Psalm 127:3-5

I want to thank my husband, Eric, for ALWAYS being there, Bethany, my happy-go-lucky songbird, for driving me to my appointments, and Shanelle (Kristen) my forever ride or die; much love. Life has not been easy for them, I know. Nonetheless, they've shown me nothing but unconditional LOVE, for which I shall be eternally grateful. Seeing that I had no trouble driving again, I was discharged from home therapy and on January 17, 2020.

I started physical therapy at our hospital's rehab center. The therapy was getting me acclimated to my new heart and a new way of living. So I would get stronger, my therapist started me out slowly on the treadmill. My amazing husband, Eric, and my extraordinary pastor's wife, Lady Samantha (Brown), as I call her, were right there with me on my very first day.

I was extremely nervous when we walked in. There were so many treadmills and people. I had never been on a treadmill. Because I was new to this, I was encouraged to go slow and work my way up; naturally, that's what I did. Furthermore, the harder I worked, the more I looked forward to going and working out.

I believe that working out is all about a mindset. Because of my dedication and determination to get better, my therapist kept moving my speed higher on the treadmill. I would set daily goals on the two machines for that day. For example, I would do 25 minutes on the treadmill and 10 to 15 minutes on the elliptical, aiming to feel better.

After a while, I was able to go out and do some things. I began attending church again for the first time since my transplant. Without a doubt, that was an exciting day for me, to be able to see all my church family that I had not seen in quite some time. Our bond as believers made this time of thankfulness so special. Although I couldn't hug everyone, they all waved, smiled, and blew kisses from a distance while tears of joy flooded my soul. We took pictures of this memorable day.

Although my health was getting better, I missed our son, Joshua, terribly and was praying for his release as his court date drew near. He continued to keep us posted on the status of his court date, as his attorney informed him. Once again, I knew it all was in the hands of the Lord, almighty. In the meantime, I decided to take a trip to Tampa, Florida, with my mom because I was doing quite well. One of her spiritual daughters, Apostle Priscilla, was asked to minister the Word of the Lord at her church. We had an amazing time lifting the name of Jesus as souls were added to the church, and lives were changing.

On our way back home, I started coughing and not feeling well, but it so happened that I had an appointment at Emory the next day, and they could run tests to check for any problems. Due to my low immune system, I had developed pneumonia and was hospitalized overnight while they gave me antibiotics. I was so fatigued and had wheezing in my chest, but after the antibiotics started to work, I began to feel somewhat better. While lying in the hospital, I talked with the Lord. I told Him, "Lord, I do not want this to be a long sickness; please heal my body." And that's exactly what He did. Eric picked me up from the hospital, and off to the house we went for me to recuperate at home.

While I was getting better, we received a letter to come to Joshua's hearing. Because I had just gotten out of the hospital, I didn't go. My husband and our pastor went, and that day will forever be remembered. Eric called to tell me that the judge did not rule on Josh's case that morning; he would have to come back after lunch. Of course, this made me feel more anxious because we were waiting, praying, and believing that he would be released that morning. Despite the news, I continued to believe God for a favorable outcome. So, the afternoon came, and Eric went back to court; time was moving on, and he finally called to say the judge was not going to release Joshua.

Now, let's take a minute to go to the Word of the Lord:

> *"Delight thyself also in the Lord, and he shall*
> *give thee the desires of thine heart."*
> Psalms 37:4

I delight to do your will Lord, is what I told the Lord, and when Eric gave me that news, I would not receive it in my spirit, knowing the prayer I had prayed. Eric then told me he would stay after court to talk with Joshua's attorney to see what our next step would be. Even though Eric had given me this news, I continued to believe God for a miracle, not knowing God had already done His part.

Eric wanted to surprise me.

Because of Eric's inability to climb stairs, he couldn't go where the court hearing was being held, so our pastor told him everything that had taken place inside the courtroom. Pastor Jackson told Eric that he knew God's favor was with Joshua as the judge gave him probation and told him he was free to go home, but he didn't want to see Joshua in his court again. So, as I sat waiting for Eric to come home, he finally enters without Joshua. We talked about the events of the day, and suddenly, Joshua comes through the door. I cried, praised God, hugged Joshua, and told Eric, "you got me good." As a family, we stayed up half the night talking, laughing, and reminiscing with Joshua.

I know what He's done for me.

CHAPTER 18

He Holds My Future

As life was moving on, the entire world faced a pandemic, causing us to experience a new normal. We were required to wear a mask when going out in public and socially distance ourselves from others. Emory felt it necessary to stop my rehab and advised me to quarantine at home with my family as a safety precaution. My life has truly been blessed with some extraordinary doctors from the cardiology department at Emory University Hospital. Dr. Andrew Smith, Wendy Book, Sonjoy Laskar, Kunal Bhatt, Maan Jokhadar, Dr. Divya Gupta, and Dr. Stacy Westerman, to name a few. They have worked extremely hard to ensure my family and I receive the best care possible. The transplant coordinators have been so supportive through the LVAD days and now the heart transplant journey. They have become a part of our family, and we love all of them. I dare not forget all of the nurses on 4E who took such great care of me and my two surgeons, whom I shall never forget, Dr. John Vega, who performed my LVAD surgery, and Dr. Tamer Attia, who performed my heart transplant surgery. They are my two Angels sent from Heaven.

Because of the pandemic, I started going to YouTube, watching different workout videos, and walking in my neighborhood to continue my healthy heart journey.

Finally, I can never repay all the people God has placed in our lives during these life-changing events. I may not have mentioned you all in this book, but God knows exactly who you are, and our prayers are with you forever. I never thought I would have experienced the things I have in my 54 years, but my experience has deepened my trust in the Lord and strengthened my relationship with Him.

I can say that Roman 8:28 is a part of my everyday life. I don't know what the future holds, but I know He holds my future in his hands. God has been faithful to me, and come what may, I will be faithful to Him.

Now, let the journey continue…

GALLERY

Eric, Teresa, Kristen, Bethany and Joshua at our
church Kingdom Life Church Ministries

Eric and Teresa Wedding Day January 28, 2001

Erin (Our Son-In Love) Erik, LaTeshia (Tia), Kristen, Bethany, Tyrun, Princess (Our Daughter-In Love) Eric, Teresa and Avah

My Mother Apostle Frances Brunson

Teresa and Tyrun at Panama City Beach Pier

Teresa Taylor Director of Children's
Friend Learning Center

LaTeshia (Tia) 3 years old and Kristen 6 months

My Assistant Tara Price

My Devotional Leader Days

My sister Sangra and her husband Darrell

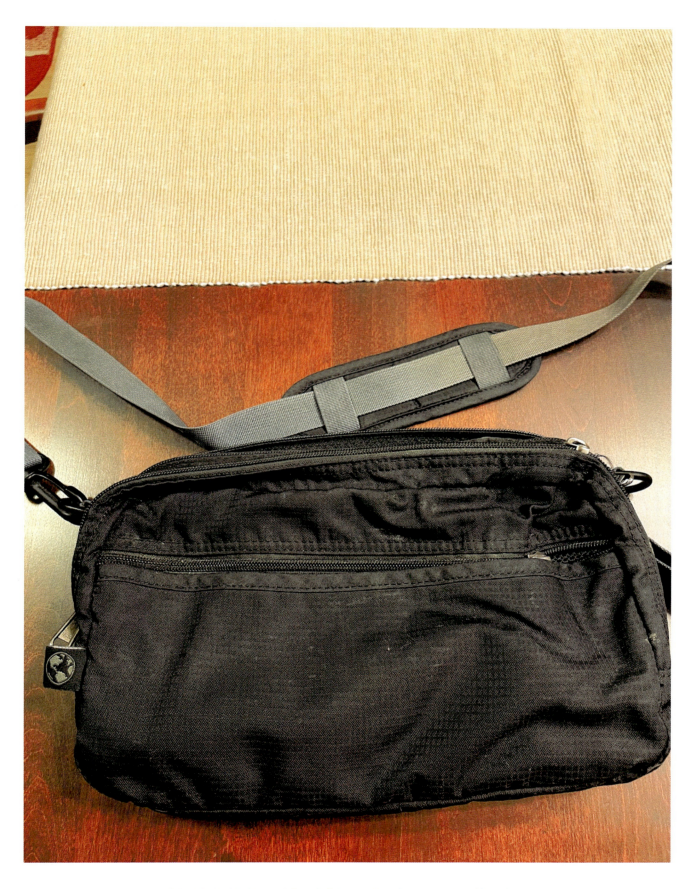

My LVAD Bag "Left Ventricular Assist Device

Me, my sister's Sangra, Betty, Tangela
and Terri with our mom

My Biological Father Woodall Terry and my Mother

Me in April of 2021, Texarkana, Texas

Me on my way to see Dr. Attia my transplant
surgeon to wish me well on my journey

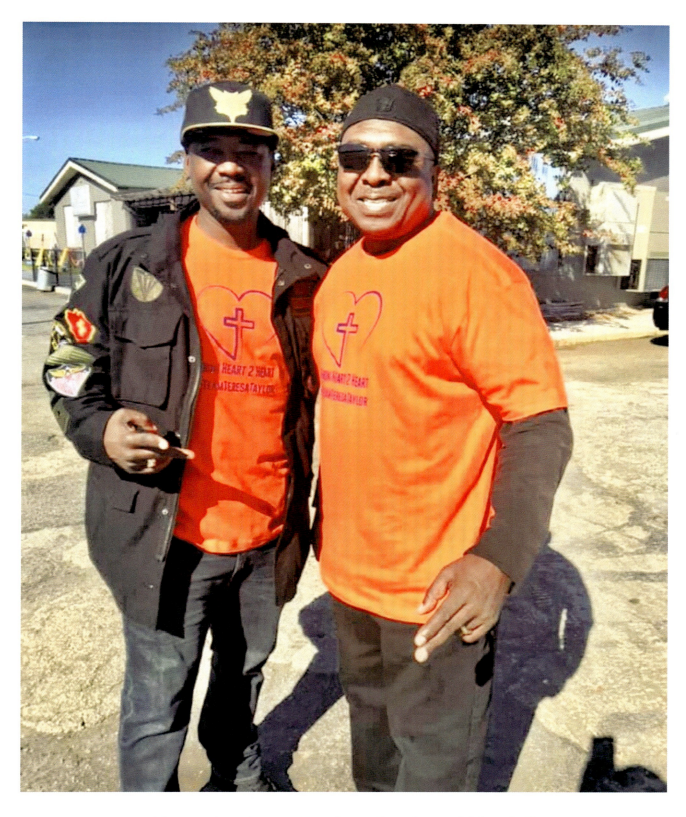

My two handsome brothers Randy and Woodall

The courtroom where Joshua was sentenced

Me and Evangelist (Pastor) Nancy

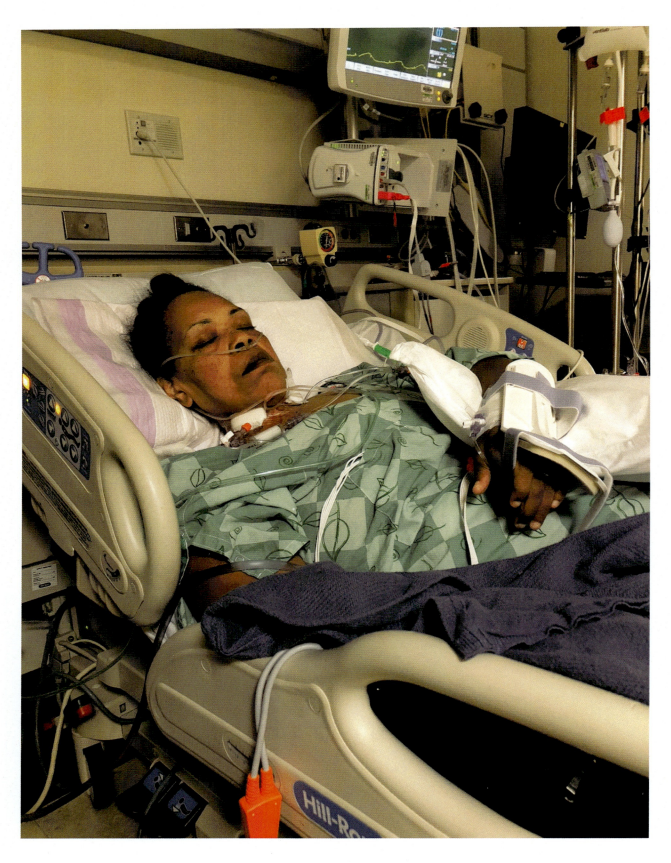

Me fighting for my life in CCU at
Emory University Hospital

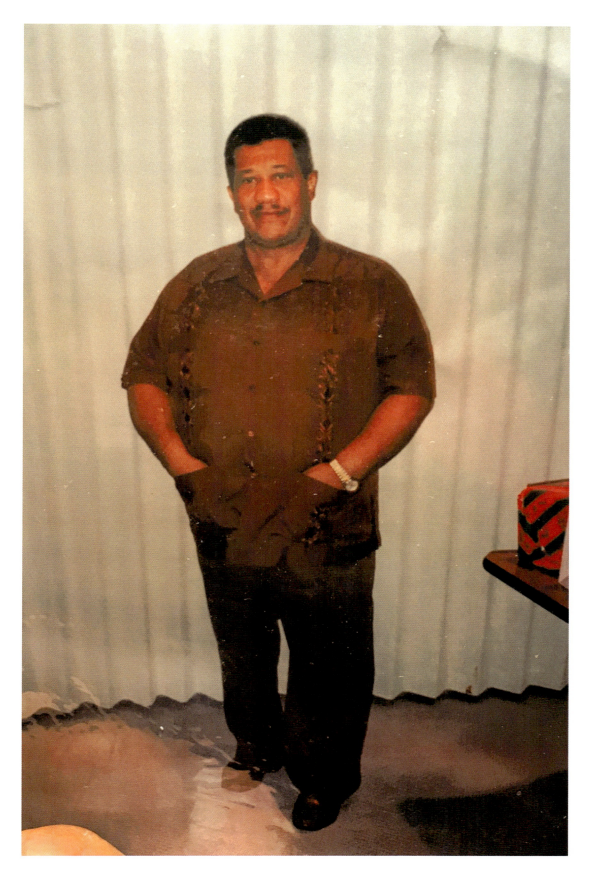

My dad The Great Apostle Robert Lee Brunson

Me in Atlanta making plans for
my cruise to the Bahamas

Me at our church

ACKNOWLEDGMENTS

Thanks, Ora Maria Marshall, for inspiring me to title my book, *The Heart Warrior. I know what He's done for me!*

Apostle Frances Brunson, my anointed mother, who NEVER gives up and NEVER STOPS PRAYING; There is no way I could ever pay you back for all you have done for me. But I want you to know you raised a Woman after God's heart. I will always treasure our mother/daughter relationship.

I love you, Ma. You are so appreciated.

To my remarkable children – Lateshia, Kristen, Lyndsay, Erik, TJ, Bethany, and Joshua; I love each of you intentionally, unconditionally, and unequivocally.

"Lo, children are a heritage of the Lord:
and the fruit of the womb is his reward."
Psalm 127:3

And I must say, Thank you, Lord, for the reward.

My Amazing Grandchildren – Quentae, Annie (My Dora), Destini, Prince, Zion, Kendrell, Kier, and my newest bundle of joy, Avah, I Love you all so much!

"TGIF This Grandma Is Fabulous" because of you ALL.

People I want to mention; My siblings; Randy, Sangra Jean (Jean), Betty, Tangela (Tan), Terri (Prophetess), and Woodall (Wood). You all have no idea the Love I have for each one of you. I am truly blessed to have you for my siblings. Aint NO siblings like the ones I got.

To my Pastor Rodney Jackson and Lady Samantha, you two have made such a great impact on my life, my family's life, and all those who meet you. Thanks for ALWAYS pushing me through the Word of God to press toward the mark of a higher calling in Christ Jesus.

Our family's favorite scripture:
"And we know that all things work together for good to them
that love God, to them who are the called according to his
purpose."
Romans 8:28

I would also like to mention my uncle, Prophet Michael Kennebrew, and Apostle Lee Tyson. These two Men of God spoke into my life on many occasions when I was hospitalized – that God would not forget about me and give me a miracle. When I was told I was being considered for placement on the transplant list, we called Apostle Tyson and told him. He said, "Woman of God, the Lord is saying when they shoot your blood type out into the data system, it will not take long before you get a heart!"-Sure enough, it only took eight days before I received my new heart.

Scripture emphasizes:
"Believe in the LORD your God, and you shall be established; believe His prophets, and you shall prosper."
2 Chronicles 20:20